Bound

Jesse Briton grew up in Somerset and trained on East 15
Acting School's Contemporary Theatre course under Uri
Roodner. His work as an actor has included performances
at Bristol Old Vic, Finborough Theatre and the ICA.
As founder and artistic director of Bear Trap Theatre
Company, he has written and directed two original works
for the company, *Bound* and *Enduring Song*, and directed
a third, *Hiraeth*. Commissioned work includes *Movere* for
Curious Directive. *Bound* is his first play, and in 2011 he
was nominated for the *Evening Standard*'s Most Promising
Playwright Award. Alongside his performance work he
regularly teaches in Somerset and London, and is a visiting
director at East 15 Acting School.

JESSE BRITON

Bound

faber and faber

First published in 2012
by Faber and Faber Limited
74–77 Great Russell Street, London WC1B 3DA

Typeset by Country Setting, Kingsdown, Kent CT14 8ES
Printed in England by CPI Group (UK) Ltd, Croydon CR0 4YY

A CIP record for this book is available from the British Library

ISBN 978-0-571-29014-7

FSC
www.fsc.org
MIX
Paper from
responsible sources
FSC® C101712

2 4 6 8 10 9 7 5 3 1

Bound was first performed as a student production as part of East 15 Acting School's Debut Festival on 6 May 2010. Its professional premiere was at Zoo Southside during the Edinburgh Fringe Festival on 6 August 2010. The original cast was as follows:

Kirk Thomas Bennett
John James Crocker
Alan James Jaggs
Graham Joe Darke
Rhys Daniel Foxsmith
Woods Jesse Briton

Director Jesse Briton
Musical Director Joe Darke

BOUND

Bound is Bear Trap Theatre Company's debut production.
It premiered at the Edinburgh Fringe Festival in 2010, winning
numerous awards during its sellout run, including a Fringe First.
Following an Australian transfer to headline the Adelaide Fringe
Festival for Holden Street Theatres, where it won the inaugural
Adelaide Advertiser Critics Choice Award and Adelaide Fringe
award for Best Performer (Ensemble), Bear Trap embarked on
a tour of the UK and Ireland with *Bound*, and was awarded the
Clonmell Junction Festival Award for Best Theatre Show. In
September 2011 the company completed a critically acclaimed
run of *Bound* at Southwark Playhouse.

AWARDS

Fringe First
Herald Angel
Herald Little Devil
NSDF and Methuen Drama Emerging Artists' Competition
Holden Street Theatres Award
Adelaide Advertiser Critics Choice Award
Adelaide Fringe Best Performer (Ensemble)
Clonmell Junction Best Theatre Show

BEAR TRAP

Bear Trap is a multi-award winning theatre company dedicated to
creating classically inspired new work. Formed in 2010 by Jesse
Briton and Joe Darke during their training with Uri Roodner on
East 15's acclaimed Contemporary Theatre course, Bear Trap
produces intimate ensemble work using epic classical narrative,
song, movement and play. Alongside their performance work Bear
Trap also run educational workshops with schools and community
groups, and provide support for emerging artists creating new
performance.

Written in the immediate aftermath of the 2008 financial crisis, *Bound* is in many ways a tale of the human cost of that event, and our response to it.

Since the industrial revolution, Britain has undergone a steady decline in areas of traditional manual skilled labour. Trades and crafts that used to be the livelihood of the majority are now the preserve of the minority, and kept alive by hardened enthusiasts. Even in recent times, technological advances, expansion of the service sector and a steady increase in globalisation have all served dramatically to hasten this decline, leaving traditional industries and those who operate them facing extinction. Trawling is one such industry.

It is remarkable that in the high-tech economy of the twenty-first century there are professions that require men and women to risk their lives on a daily basis for the provision of something so basic and essential as food – and more specifically, fish. In those communities along our coastline that provide us with this food source, you would be hard pressed to find an individual who has not lost a relative or friend to tragedy at sea. A reality that is tragedy is matched only by its sad regularity. Yet in the face of such heartbreaking loss, it is clear that in these communities their shared trauma is held as a mark of pride.

We are reminded that written throughout this island's history are the successes and failures of its seafarers; the sheer range of nautical terminology used in the modern lexicon remains testament to this. These individuals and the industry they form can be seen as one of the single greatest shaping influences on modern Britain. But despite their clear significance, we remain oblivious to the individuals who continue this work, in an industry that has remained fundamentally unchanged for hundreds of years.

Bound examines the effect of these pressures on one small group of Brixham trawlermen, and their boat, the *Violet*.

Bound was born and developed by Jesse Briton while still a student, for the Debut Festival, part of a unique actor training programme at East 15 Acting School just outside London – the BA in Acting and Contemporary Theatre, or 'CT' as its alumni like to call it.

The CT course is renowned not only as an innovative and highly influential actor training programme, but also as a creative hub that has, in its short history (established 2003), produced innovative theatrical work that has transferred to venues worldwide. The training is dedicated to the development of an emerging actor training methodology that focuses on innovation and the creation of original graduate work. This approach is underpinned by a philosophy that sees the actor as an independent, creative and entrepreneurial 'artist'. The programme attracts multi-talented performers who want to experiment, explore and participate as 'actor-creators'.

Uri Roodner, who leads the course, has brought to it inspirations from actor-led companies such as Theatre de Complicite, Kneehigh and Improbable Theatre. He was aware that while work produced on the course was often strong on image and concept, there were weaknesses at times in structure and the use of language. The course became revolutionary when he invited playwright April De Angelis to lead a writing component in the training. In her class actors experiment with playwriting, and some of the plays developed during this process are picked to receive full production treatment as part of the annual Debut Festival, put together in collaboration with Paul Warwick of China Plate.

All the Debut Festival plays are staged by first-time writers, directors and producers who are students on the CT course. Since the project's inauguration in 2008 a number of Debut plays have gone on to professional production, appearing at the Edinburgh Festival, the Brighton Festival, and touring with companies (who like Bear Trap were established during training) to numerous theatres in Britain and abroad. The relationship between these companies of graduates and the course often continue after graduation, and many come back to develop their new work with students on the course. Direct collaborations between the course and established companies have developed and include work with the National Theatre Studio, Soho Theatre and the London South Bank Centre.

ACKNOWLEDGEMENTS

Bear Trap would like to thank April De Angelis, Holly Kendrick and the NSDF, Ed Collier and Paul Warwick of China Plate, Marcin Rudy, Colin Sadler, East 15 Acting School and Uri Roodner.

Characters

Woods
skipper of the the *Violet*,
premier of a dying empire

John
school friend of Woods,
left behind by life

Rhys
Welsh; missed out on a university education

Alan
'too weak to do anything physical, too old to cook'

Graham
handsome enough to know every girl in Brixham,
young enough to enjoy it

Kerdzic
entrepreneurial Polish agency worker

Matt
(voice)
skipper of the *New Hope*

With the exception of Scene One
(set in Brixham Harbour), the action takes place
aboard the *Violet*, an ageing fishing trawler
working out of Brixham

BOUND

Songs

The Last Leviathan

Roll Down

South Australia

The Greenland Whale Fishery

Lowlands

Paddy Doyle's Boots

Leave Her, Johnny

Hand over Hand

Can't You Dance the Polka?

The cast sing from 'The Last Leviathan' by Andy Barnes.

Brixham Harbour. Early morning. Kerdzic enters. He looks around, drops his bag to the floor and removes a letter from his pocket. John enters. The two men stand next to each other.

John Morning.

Kerdzic Good morning.

Pause.

John It's going to rain later.

Beat.

I can feel it.

Pause.

Kerdzic Are you Woods?

John No.

Beat.

Why you looking for him?

Kerdzic Work.

Beat.

John He hasn't got any.

Kerdzic He needs workers.

Beat.

John I don't think he does.

Kerdzic I have to go with Woods on the *Wiolet*.

John The *Violet*?

Kerdzic I have to go with Woods on the *Wiolet*.

John No, it's called the *Violet*.

Kerdzic I'm here to work. I have paper.

Kerdzic removes a folded piece of paper from his pocket and reads from it.

'The *Wiolet* leaves at five o'clock from the West Dock. Take your permit and a change of clothes. Transport is provided to the dock at additional cost and will be deducted from your pay. Do not steal anything. They will feed you. This will be deducted also. Ask for Woods. He is skipper. Do not steal anything.'

Pause. Kerdzic looks expectantly at John. John extends his hand for the paper.

John Here.

Kerdzic hands him the paper. He studies it for a moment. Sighs and shakes his head.

(*To himself.*) Bloody agency. (*Over-articulating.*) Read my lips. *This* is wrong. We came back from a haul last night, alright? Fish? You understand fish? They swim in the ocean. (*Mimes fish.*) We caught big bagfuls of them, make a lot of money, now we go on holiday. Ho-li-day. No work today. The agency have sent you to the wrong place.

Kerdzic The agency said come here today. Five o'clock.

John No. Not five o'clock. No o'clock.

Kerdzic I don't understand. Are you Woods?

John No, I'm not Woods. You Polish?

Kerdzic Yes.

John Do you have a phone? You need to call the agency.

Kerdzic I don't have a phone.

John There's one up at the house you can use.

John points towards the house. Alan enters.

Alan John.

John Morning, Alan.

Alan Who's your friend?

John He's from the agency.

Beat.

Alan Rhys'll like that.

John Hopefully he'll be gone by then.

Alan For his own sake. What's he doing here?

John Agency have sent him to the wrong place.

Alan Silly buggers.

John Have you got a phone he can borrow?

Alan No.

John (*to Kerdzic*) You'll have to go up to the house.

Kerdzic I will wait here.

John That's not the best idea, mate.

Alan He's Polish?

John Aye.

Alan 'Ere, no fishing to be done in Poland, was there?

5

Alan laughs.

John You should get out of here before Rhys arrives.

Kerdzic I was told to wait.

John Please yourself.

Alan Silly bugger.

John Aye.

Alan You been paid yet?

John He's running late.

Alan Got any plans for it?

John Straight into the bank. Yours?

Alan Cumberland sausage.

John laughs.

I'm going to buy all the Cumberland sausage I can find. I'm going to eat half of it, then the other half I'm going to sit and look at. Whatever money I have left will go to Simon. Him and his girlfriend are looking for a house.

John Already? How old is he now?

Alan Twenty-one.

John They grow up, don't they . . . ?

Alan We're very proud of him.

Pause.

John Was it his idea or hers?

Beat.

Alan I don't know.

Pause.

John Tell him to go careful with her.

Alan I think he'll be alright, John.

John Women at that age don't really care about your feelings, they only care about themselves. They pretend well, but under the surface it's all want and despair. Like a big black hole. I guess you could say that about women of any age, though. Perhaps they get more cunning the older they get, or the more desperate?

Alan I'll pass on your regards.

Graham enters, startling John and Alan.

Graham All hands on deck!

John Christ, Graham!

Alan Little – (*bastard*).

Graham Don't have a heart attack, Alan.

Graham limps his way on. He is crouched, head hung and missing a jacket.

John You look a state.

Graham I'm not going to lie to you, John. I am hungover. In fact I think I'm still drunk, I think I've got a drunk-over.

John We only got back eight hours ago.

Graham In that case I'm just drunk.

Alan What happened to your leg?

Graham seats himself awkwardly on the floor.

Graham I fell off a bollard.

Alan Where?

Graham Top of a hill.

Alan Which hill?

Graham Alan! Can you stop asking me questions? I just told you I'm hungover. (*Seeing Kerdzic.*) Who the hell is that?

John He's from the agency.

Graham He's beautiful. Has Rhys seen him?

John Not yet.

Graham Oh dear, oh dear. He's going to break his legs.

John Hopefully he'll be gone by then.

Graham Oh, I'm excited now. How long's he been here for?

John Five minutes.

Graham What's his name?

John and Alan look at each other.

You haven't asked him his name?

Silence.

Honestly, boys, where's your manners gone . . .

He looks at them with exaggerated disapproval.

Hello . . . my name's Graham. What's your name then?

Kerdzic Kerdzic.

Beat.

Graham That's a beautiful name. Well done, really well done. It's a pleasure to meet you. What you up to then, big man? Eh? Because I'm here collecting money. What's that, you ask? Where is my money? I dunno, let's ask Grumpy and Bashful. Right, boys, where's the pay? Come on, hand it over, we've got some fun to be had!

Pats Kerdzic's head.

John He's running late.

Graham Jesus Christ! I'm a busy man you know, I can't spend all my life hanging round these bloody docks.

Alan I notice your jacket's missing?

Graham I gave it to a girl, didn't I.

Alan You're not cold?

Graham Do you want to give me yours?

An argument begins. In the distance we see Rhys enter.

Rhys Alright, boys, don't panic, the Welsh is here!

Rhys wades in, separating the two parties. Graham continues bickering as Rhys tries to calm him down, suddenly Kerdzic interrupts.

Kerdzic Are you Woods?

Pause.

Rhys Who's this?

Pause.

What are you doing here?

Kerdzic I'm here to work.

Rhys Where?

Kerdzic The *Wiolet*.

John *Violet.*

Beat.

Rhys You missed it, pal, we arrived back yesterday.

Kerdzic I'm waiting for Woods.

Rhys We all are, by the look of things.

Rhys turns away, the others naturally follow. He pauses and turns back.

From the agency, are we?

The others tense up. Graham exhales audibly.

Kerdzic The agency sent me.

Rhys Did they now?

Pause.

How much are you on then?

John Rhys . . .

Kerdzic I don't understand.

John Just ignore him.

Rhys Let him answer.

John It's too early for this.

Rhys No, that's what they want you to think, John. How much you on then?

Kerdzic I don't understand . . .

Rhys Money. Sterling. How much? Go on, you can tell us, we're only the poor boys you're undercutting. How much is it? Seventy a day? No, fifty? That sound right?

Kerdzic looks confused.

Kerdzic I'm not here to fight.

Rhys Whoa! Hang on a minute! Who said anything about fighting? I never said anything about fighting! Graham, did you say anything about fighting? Alan, you say anything about fighting? John? John! John's always fighting, in' 'e. He loves it. Can't get enough of it! No, I'm not going to fight you. I should. Now tell me, and be honest, as you were signing that agency form – the one that says I have no qualms with driving the indigenous labour out of work and destroying any union they might have – did you think of me?

Kerdzic I don't know you.

Rhys Yes you do, you liar. Because I know you. I know that when you send your pay cheque home it's worth double what it is here. I know that your family aren't starving and you're not doing this for them. I also know that when this job is finished, when you lot have had your fill and bled us dry, you'll hop back on your planes and leave us with nothing. This money will buy you a nice house, won't it? Maybe a car? Or if it stretches that far, even a fancy laptop computer?

John He's not starting anything.

Rhys Neither am I, we're just having a chat, aren't we?

Kerdzic I have a paper.

Rhys (*starting to lose it*) Oh! He's got a paper!

They move into Rhys's path, and ease him away.

John Easy now, come on.

Rhys Back on your plane, mate.

John Rhys . . .

Rhys It's alright, John. It's alright. Happy families here.

Graham Well done, Rhys, that was like an advert for equality.

Rhys Morning, Graham. God, you smell awful! Carried on the night alone then, I see?

Graham I can find you a couple of girls who would say very different, couple of guys as well, Alan, if you're interested?

Winks at Alan.

Rhys I doubt that. I left you at what . . . one? Where'd you go after that?

Graham Everywhere. I went everywhere, Rhys, and you missed out. Time of my life it was. But that ain't important. What is important is that I'm here now with you and I'll never leave you again, mate. I promise. Never again. I love you.

Rhys Are you planning on spending the rest of your holiday in this state?

Graham I'm planning on spending the rest of my life in this state.

Alan We'll see.

Graham Alan? Are you talking to me?

Alan Couple of pints and look at you.

Graham Alright, what are you going to do with the rest of your holiday? Take up line-dancing?

Alan It's not line-dancing! It's ballroom. Classical. It takes a lot of finesse and skill.

Graham So does wanking . . .

Alan That's the reason why you won't amount to anything. You want to know something about dancing?

Graham No.

Alan Listen here, you might learn something. Dancing's about control, understanding, communication between two people. It's what being a man is all about, not a feckless halfwit teenager.

Graham Oh, I'm in the company of men now, am I?

John Gentlemen . . .

Graham Don't worry, John, I'm going back to bed.

Graham settles himself back on the floor.

Rhys I went past the bakery this morning, Graham . . .

Rhys gives Graham a light kick.

Graham Did you?

Rhys Your mother was very upset. She was expecting to see you when you got in.

Beat.

Graham Don't do it, Rhys . . .

Beat.

Rhys She offered me a lovely pair of . . .

Graham RHYS! Don't talk about my mother!

John Gentlemen . . .

Graham My mother's a saint!

Graham struggles to his feet. Rhys is already moving away from him as he starts to give chase. Graham struggles to remove his welly in the hope of launching it at Rhys.

Rhys He's up now!

As Graham continues to pursue Rhys, with Alan caught between them, Woods enters.

Woods John.

John Woods.

Woods I'm glad to see you.

John What's going on?

Woods Is everyone here?

John And one extra. Something happen?

Woods Follow my lead, John. Right, gather round. I'm sorry about this, lads, I know you were all on break. Are you from the agency?

Kerdzic I came in a van.

Woods I asked for two, where's your driver?

Kerdzic He's gone.

Graham Hit and run.

Rhys What's he doing here?

Pause.

Woods After we returned last night, I moved the catch into the market hall ready for this morning. We're all boxed up and ready for the bidding when the market doors open and no one appears. We wait a good couple of hours, twiddling our bloody thumbs, until this call comes through to the office. We all crowd in round the phone and there's this young chap on the other end from our biggest regional buyer, saying he's the commercial purchases consultant assistant or some bollocks. He says the company's gone into administration. They've stopped all trading. There won't be anyone buying fish today.

Beat.

John They're bankrupt?

Woods It appears so.

Beat.

Rhys What about the other buyers?

Beat.

Woods There were some independents that showed up later. Course, everyone jumped on them, flogging whole catches for a quarter of market price. It was embarrassing, you got skippers back there crying in corners. Now you'll be grateful to know I was able to sell our lot. But we're still under by a bit.

Alan How much?

Beat.

Woods Ten grand.

Graham That's cheap.

Woods You're lucky I sold it at all.

Rhys What about pay?

Woods We're looking into it. The girls are in the office working their way through everything as we speak, it's complicated.

Beat.

Graham Well, this all sounds like terrible news. It really does. I'll just take my money now, and you boys can sort this out . . .

Pause.

Hang on . . . oh no . . . oh no, mate . . .

Beat.

No, no, no. I'm not hearing this. Tell me I'm not hearing this!

Beat.

You don't have the money, do you? You've run out of bloody money?

Woods We need to go back out.

Graham You're going out again?

Woods We all are.

Graham That's a bad idea.

Woods Why?

Graham We've just got back. I'm hammered.

Woods You can sober up on board.

Alan We were on a holiday.

Woods I know. I'm sorry.

Alan I had plans.

Woods Dancing plans?

Pause.

Alan Yes.

Woods Come on, lads.

Woods and John move to exit.

John, can you get her . . .

Rhys Does the union know about this? About us going out?

Beat.

Woods No one does.

Rhys Right. You'll have to find someone else.

Rhys starts to walk away.

Woods Hang on.

Rhys I don't work for free, mate, sorry.

Graham I'm coming with you.

Graham makes to join Rhys.

Woods The union can't know.

Rhys We have a union to protect us from this. This and that bloody lot – (*Points to Kerdzic.*)

Graham Yeah!

Alan Shut up, Graham.

Woods No one can find out. We've got an opportunity here. If the others figure it out then our chance is lost.

Alan Figure what out?

Woods No one saw this coming, right? And everyone's been hit hard by it. Very badly in some cases. I dare say there'll be a few boats scrapped by the end of the day. But there's still a market, and they still need fish. Now you lot imagine if we're the only ones to pull up with a boatload of fish as the doors re-open. We'll be kings. Premium rate, double the price on everything! And if the other skippers are sat in dock trying to work out how to pay their crews, they won't be out catching.

Graham Maybe you should be doing that as well.

John Listen to him.

Woods It's simple. We go out today and we're the only ones. We have monopoly on the market.

Pause.

John I'll go.

Graham John!

John It's not a bad idea.

Graham It's not a good idea! Of course you're going to go, you're his mate.

Alan It's not a bad idea.

Graham Come on, Alan. You're just saying that because he said it.

Alan I am not. I'm a fisherman. I'm meant to be out there, not sitting around here crying. Just another day as far as I'm concerned. I'll have to ring the wife.

Woods Not a problem.

Graham Rhys, let's do one.

No response.

(*To Kerdzic.*) 'Ere, Popeye, you coming?

John He's on agency pay, he's staying.

Pause.

Woods Come on, mate.

Rhys Don't screw me about.

Woods I'm not.

Beat.

Rhys I need that money.

Woods You'll get it. I promise.

Beat.

Graham Rhys?

Beat.

Rhys Hannah won't be happy.

Woods They never are.

Graham Rhys! Don't do this, mate. I look like a proper one now!

John Are you coming?

Graham No.

Graham considers his position as the others climb aboard.

Double pay?

John laughs.

I'm not going. I'm going home. I'm going home and I'm going to have a shag instead because this is just . . .

John laughs again and follows the others on board.

Bollocks.

Exit.

The cast sing from 'Roll Down' by Peter Bellamy (from The Transports).

SCENE TWO

The deck. The silhouette of Brixham is faintly visible as it slips out of view. The light is low and the sky in front is red. The ocean sits calmly. The crew are watching as the nets are dragged in.

Alan I'll never get tired of seeing that.

John How much?

Alan One-eighty.

Pause.

Graham Now?

Alan It's coming!

Rhys Come on.

The nets shudder to a halt.

Alan We're jammed!

John (*to wheelhouse*) Dead stop! Dead stop!

Rhys Balls.

Kerdzic Is the boat broken?

Graham The net's caught.

Kerdzic On what?

Graham Could be anything. Too high to be the seabed, might be a wreck.

Alan It won't come in any.

Rhys We can pedal on, try and tear it free?

Alan Rip the net free?

Rhys Unless someone wants to swim down and cut it, we're not going anywhere.

Kerdzic I can swim.

John That's not what he meant.

Graham Go for it, Kirk!

  Kerdzic removes his jumper.

Alan Graham, shut up.

John Put your jumper back on, Kirk.

Graham He just wants to help.

Rhys It's your decision, John.

  Beat.

John (*to wheelhouse*) Start her up again!

  The net is hauled in and hangs above them, ripped.

  (*To wheelhouse.*) The net's ripped!

Alan That's four grand down the drain.

Kerdzic To repair the net?

Alan Catch on quickly, don't you?

John We shouldn't have ripped it free.

Rhys It's done now.

Graham Serves us right for hauling so close to shore.

John Now you want to go further out? I thought you didn't want to come?

Graham I still don't.

Alan I knew this trip was cursed.

Graham You've changed your tune.

Alan I'm just saying.

Kerdzic Why is it cursed?

Alan I'm not going to explain everything to him!

Graham I think it's cursed too.

John No one wants to hear it, gentlemen.

Alan Bound to happen. Going out on a whim, unprepared like this. You shouldn't disrespect the sea. Luck will always be batting for her team. I've been on more than a few cursed ships, you know.

Graham I can believe that, Alan.

John This doesn't help anyone.

Rhys How many nets do we have left?

John It's not important.

    Pause. Rhys looks at John.

Let's just get this away.

Rhys It would be useful to know how many nets we have.

John Come on.

Rhys John. How many nets do we have left?

John . . .

Rhys Graham?

Graham What's that then, mate?

Rhys John won't tell me how many nets we have left.

Graham Why won't he tell you how many nets we have left?

John Gentlemen . . .

Graham How many nets we got left, Jonno?

John . . .

Graham Alan, John won't tell us how many nets are left.

Alan Why?

Graham Mental breakdown?

Alan How many nets are left, John?

John remains stubbornly silent.

Rhys I'm going to look.

John We've got three nets left.

Beat.

Graham Three?

Alan That'll be the curse.

Graham Why do we only have three nets left?

John There wasn't enough money to replace the last one when we had to cut it loose.

Graham What kind of a catch are we going to have with three bloody nets?

John We were selling the other boats off at the time. We just lost Lizzie and there wasn't enough money for a new net.

Alan Lizzie was a good boat.

Graham So he lost us a boat and net.

John And himself a bloody awful lot of money, but I don't see that troubling you!

Graham Language, John.

John I'm sorry.

Graham You are forgiven. Long day. (*Pats him on the back.*) Stay sexy, mate.

Alan Cursed. This is how they start.

John Can we please talk about something else?

Rhys Take it easy, John. Happy families here.

Rhys turns his attention to Graham.

Hey, Graham! Hey, big man!

Graham What?

Rhys I spoke to your mother this morning.

Graham Don't start, Rhys, I'm about ready to jump off this boat.

Rhys It was a good chat we had. Healthy like.

Graham I didn't see her before we come out. She'll be going mental right now.

Alan Miss your mummy, Graham?

Graham Eat my arse, Alan.

Rhys She's worried about you, mate. She said she wanted you to settle down with one of these girls that you're seeing. She didn't say which one, mind, just any of them would do.

Graham Not interested. Besides, it would be a crime to chain this body to a single woman. Love is balls anyway.

Rhys How little you know.

Graham Coming from the man whose marriage is failing?

Beat.

Rhys That's different.

Graham How?

Rhys Life changes people. Marriage certainly does. And we're not great at dealing with change, us humans. I know, and I'm better than most. Hannah may not love me the way she once did, but, you know, it gets hard. You should never disregard love, young man, you just don't understand what it is yet. But you'll learn that.

Beat.

Graham You wet bastard. Right, here are some examples. John. Divorced. Wife ran off with another man.

John This isn't what I meant by talk of something else.

Graham Woods. Divorced. With a son he had to look after by himself. Alan, still with his wife, and look at him . . .

Alan Excuse me?

Graham Explains a lot, doesn't it? And Kirk. Kirk, you have a lady in Poland?

Kerdzic Jozef.

Graham See, even Kirk has a girlfriend, yet he feels the need to come all the way out here to England, hundreds of miles away from her. Speaks for itself.

Their attention falls on Kerdzic.

Alan Polish?

Kerdzic Yes?

Alan We're packing the nets.

Kerdzic Yes?

Pause. Incredulous looks from Alan . . .

Alan Don't you want to get paid?

Kerdzic Can I speak to my brother?

Beat.

Alan I knew we shouldn't have brought this idiot, I told you he's crazy.

John Maybe he means the sea, perhaps it's a Polish thing.

Kerdzic suddenly starts jumping up and down. Waving excitedly.

Graham Kirk?

Alan Don't talk to him, I don't want him on this boat.

Graham Stop breathing my air, you idle . . .

Alan If it's anyone's air . . .

John Gentlemen . . .

Alan and Graham start bickering, John moves in to separate them.

Rhys (*to Woods*) This is exactly what I'm talking about, Woods, how many times have I told you! I know they're cheap but its not worth it, mate!

Rhys moves to see what Kerdzic is waving at.

Kerdzic (*pointing out to sea*) There.

Rhys What?

Rhys squints in the direction Kerdzic is pointing. John tries to calm the ongoing brawl between Graham and Alan. Suddenly Rhys's demeanour changes, his voice becoming urgent.

John. You need to see this.

John pushes his way between the quarrelling Alan and Graham. He looks in the direction Rhys is now pointing.

John The *New Hope.*

Rhys You sure?

John That size, it has to be.

John turns and shouts towards the wheelhouse.

Woods!

His shout is drowned out by Graham and Alan's squabbling.

Rhys Graham, shut up!

Graham He started it!

Rhys Both of you – quiet!

Alan Don't tell me what to do.

John Woods!

Rhys Graham.

Graham What?

Rhys Alan.

John *New Hope.*

The argument stops. All move to Kerdzic.

Alan How long have they been there?

Kerdzic They left this morning.

John How do you know that?

Kerdzic My brother's on that boat.

Rhys Your brother's on the *New Hope*?

Kerdzic Yes, his name is Jozef. He left this morning.

Rhys That would have been useful to know before.

Kerdzic He was very excited.

Alan I bet he was.

Beat.

Kerdzic Why are you upset?

Alan Competition's arrived.

John Your brother's on one of the biggest trawlers in the south-west.

Rhys And fastest.

Alan Crew of twenty plus. Very efficient boat.

Graham They've probably got more than three nets.

John If they catch and get back first we're done.

Rhys It's a race then.

Alan Here they come . . . Look at the speed on that thing.

They fall into the towering shadow of the other ship. Graham opens a dialogue with the new arrivals.

Graham 'Ere, boys!

John Don't start this.

Graham Pull over, let's have a chat, shall we?

John Let's be civil, gentlemen.

Graham I've got a cock bigger than that boat!

> *Reactions from John and Alan.*

John Oh God, not again . . .

Rhys Here we go!

Alan Graham!

Rhys It's business time.

John Graham . . .

Graham Have a look at this . . .

> *Graham removes his penis from his trousers and waves it provocatively at the other boat.*

Oi! Oi! That's a real sailor penis! We don't all need big bloody boats!

John Put that away!

Graham I'm the king of the world! Get your cock out, John!

John I'm not doing that.

Rhys Go on, John!

John No!

Graham Get your chap out, Alan!

Alan I'd rather chop it off.

Graham Let's get the hose!

John No!

Alan Disgusting.

Graham Get the hose! Let's spray them!

John No!

The other boat begins to pull away.

Graham Yeah, jog on!

The shadow of the other ship passes and they all watch as it moves away.

Alan That changes things.

Rhys I think we won that one.

John Can we get these away?

> In South Australia I was born, to me heave
>   away, haul away,
> In South Australia round Cape Horn, and
>   we're bound for South Australia,
> Haul away you rolling kings, to me heave
>   away, haul away,
> Haul away you'll hear me sing and we're
>   bound for South Australia.

SCENE THREE

The galley. A single table and clutch of chairs. Alan, Graham and Rhys are seated.

Alan What's wrong?

Graham Nothing.

Alan You have a problem with me?

Graham No.

Alan If there's a problem then spit it out.

Beat.

Graham Alright.

Alan Good.

Graham Alright, you're lazy.

Alan What?

Graham You are, you're bloody lazy.

Alan Watch your mouth now.

Graham No, you asked, now I'm telling you. You're lazy. You get up half an hour later than us. You take three times as many breaks. You're greedy, you always have a portion and a half for dinner.

Alan I cook it.

Graham Only so you don't have to be boxing up.

Alan I'm the cook.

Graham Korma from a can? I can cook that.

Alan Sod off.

Graham Burger and chips? Frozen? Not much of a challenge, is it? And nobody complains?

Rhys Don't look at me.

Graham Am I not right?

Rhys Not getting involved.

Alan You're a little boy. That's all you are, a little boy out here in a big ocean. Do you know that? You want to know how long I've been doing this?

Graham Eighty years?

Alan Thirty-one year.

Beat.

Graham And how many of those were you cook for?

Alan Come here! I'll break you!

Alan rushes towards him. Graham avoids artfully. Alan circles round the table in pursuit.

Rhys Easy now!

Rhys attempts to hold Alan back.

Alan Get away from me!

Alan pushes him out of his way.

Rhys Christ . . .

Alan (*lunging at Graham*) Come here!

Graham Thirty-one years and not skipper?

Alan By choice!

Graham Not even first mate?

Alan Give me that!

Alan picks up Rhys's hat and begins swinging it wildly, before succumbing to exhaustion.

I don't have to justify myself to you. I don't. I won't.

Graham Yes you do, you still get a bigger cut than us.

Alan I'm more experienced.

Graham Oldest.

Alan You're still young, so let me tell you something: out here we don't have laws.

Graham We have rules.

Alan We have traditions. No policeman will come out here to nick you. Nobody cares about us unless we don't come back or we come back with nothing.

Graham You're still bloody lazy.

Alan You have no idea what it takes to do this job.

Graham Yes I do. You think that just because you've been doing this for a hundred years that you can do piss-all work, and from what I've heard you've always been like that.

Alan Who told you that?

Graham Loads of people.

Alan Give me names.

Graham There's too many to list.

Alan I've been trawling the whole of my working life, my father did it before me and his father before him.

Graham Yeah, I've heard things about your father and all.

Beat.

Alan You say one word about my father . . .

Rhys Graham . . .

Graham *Glory.*

Alan is frozen to the spot.

Rhys Graham . . .

Graham I know. Listen to you spouting on about your family like I don't know who your dad was. Like the whole of Brixham doesn't know. You're right about one thing – long memories. Eight men on the *Glory*? All drowned. Bar one. Your dad. Skipper. Going out into a storm, panicked. Steered the ship right into land. Not exactly an easy mistake to make. I mean, you'd think he'd know where the bloody coast was.

Alan rushes at Graham, Rhys steps between them.

Alan I'm going to kill you.

Graham Like father, like son?

They continue to grapple with each other. Woods enters. Rhys is able to separate them.

Rhys Easy, boys . . .

Woods What the hell is going on?

Alan I'm going to have you one day, when your boyfriend isn't here to hold your hand!

Alan storms out.

Woods Don't you think we've got enough to bloody deal with?

Rhys Just a quick game of rugby.

Woods Sort yourselves out!

Pause. Woods calms himself.

Where's that Polish boy gone?

Rhys John's got him cleaning nets.

Woods Clean this place up. Bloody mess.

Woods storms out.

Rhys This is turning into a fun trip. Went for the jugular there, didn't we?

Graham What use is he? He's too weak to do anything physical and too old to cook. And – I have no idea how this one works – he's afraid of sailing.

Rhys Only steering.

Graham He won't go in the wheelhouse.

Rhys It's trauma.

Graham Too right it's trauma. What if something happened and he needed to take the wheel? He'd crap himself, I'm telling you . . . crap would go everywhere.

Rhys He's got a point about the pay.

Graham You're on his side?

Rhys You won't be complaining about it in twenty years' time.

Graham I won't be here in twenty years' time.

Rhys Right.

Graham Right.

Rhys Let me tell you something here, Graham.

Rhys sits.

Graham What's that?

Rhys We need to look out for each other out here. There's no security in this. No health care, no company car. You finish your day's work and instead of going home you bunk down with a group of stinking chaps for a night. On and on. Day after day. Who's going to look after you other than us? Who gives a sod?

Graham Shouldn't get paid more.

Rhys So we should just ditch him? After all the years he's done?

Graham Yes. I wouldn't be here if I couldn't carry weight.

Rhys You think you're here because you can carry weight?

Beat.

Graham I got this job fairly.

Rhys The way you act you wouldn't have kept it for long. I guarantee you that.

Beat.

Graham Don't be such a wise arse. I know what you're thinking and that ain't it.

Beat.

Rhys You know what he'd give to be in your boots? He's had one night in his father's life hanging round his neck since he was a child. One awful bloody night. Your father . . .

Graham My father never did anything for me when he was alive and he's not taking credit for it now. You're all the same. Respect for the dead. Well done to him going out in a storm. What a brave man. Embodying the spirit of the job. Down with the ship and all that. Worthless as his father may have been, at least he made it back.

Rhys It's not undeserved credit.

Graham Knew him well, did you? Knew what he was like at home?

Rhys As a matter of fact . . .

Graham The man was a loser. And he was worshipped in death. I don't want any more said on it by stupid old men who miss their youth.

Rhys As you wish.

Pause.

The one thing I hate about my father, is that he got to my mother first.

Beat. Rhys looks deep into Graham's eyes.

Graham No, Rhys. I'm not in the mood.

Rhys Come on, baby, let me in.

Graham I don't want to.

Rhys Yes you do.

Graham No.

Rhys I love you.

   Beat.

Say it.

   Beat.

Say it.

   Beat.

Graham I love you too.

Rhys Stop it, you're embarrassing me. Kiss me.

Graham I'm not kissing you.

Rhys (*rising from his chair*) Alright. But I'm coming for you later. Just me and you, alone, in the cabin.

Graham Sod off.

Rhys Good boy.

   Rhys exits. Graham alone.

> They took us jolly sailor lads
> A-fishing for the whale.
> On the fourth day of August in 1864
> Bound for Greenland we set sail.

SCENE FOUR

The wheelhouse. Woods stands alone playing nervously with a hand-held radio. Kerdzic enters. Woods pockets the radio.

Kerdzic Captain? I was told you wanted to speak to me.

Woods Yes, come in. What's your name?

Kerdzic Kerdzic.

Woods The others call you Kirk?

Kerdzic Yes.

Woods Have a seat, Kirk.

Kerdzic sits.

Make yourself comfortable. You need anything? Drink, or something?

Kerdzic No thank you.

Woods How are you finding England?

Beat.

Kerdzic How did I find England?

Woods Yeah.

Kerdzic I came on the plane.

Beat. Woods laughs, Kerdzic looks confused.

Woods You're a funny man, Kirk. Got a good sense of humour. I like that. You getting on well with everyone? Having any problems fitting in? Because that's what I'm here for, Kirk. Any trouble and you just let me know, mate, you let me know and I'll sort it out, alright?

Kerdzic Thank you.

Woods Not a problem, Kirk. That's my job.

Pause.

They tell me you've got a brother, Kirk?

Kerdzic Jozef.

Woods Joseph, that's right. He's on the *New Hope*, isn't he?

Kerdzic Yes.

Woods He left with them this morning?

Kerdzic Yes.

Woods And he was in the same van as you?

Kerdzic Yes.

    Beat.

Woods Did you know he was meant to be with us?

Kerdzic He had different papers.

    Beat.

Woods He was meant to be with us. It doesn't matter. Not a problem, Kirk, not a problem. But you mentioned his papers, what did his papers say?

Kerdzic I don't know.

Woods It say when he was returning?

Kerdzic I don't know. I didn't look at them.

    Beat.

Woods Had he spoken to Matt?

Kerdzic He did not say. I don't know. I don't know who Matt is.

Woods OK. Did he mention anything about a direction? Where they may have been headed?

Kerdzic He did not know.

Woods You don't know or he didn't know?

Kerdzic Him.

Woods You are certain?

Kerdzic The papers never say.

Pause.

Woods You come to Brixham with your brother, didn't you?

Kerdzic It was my brother's idea to come to England. He has done a lot of fishing before. He said it was easy, he would show me what to do. I need the money. I'm building a company.

Pause.

Woods Kirk, did Matt pay more to get your brother?

Kerdzic We are paid the same. I don't know who Matt is.

Woods Has the agency told you to lie to me?

Kerdzic No.

Woods Did they give you money?

Kerdzic No.

Woods Did Matt give you money?

Kerdzic I don't know who Matt is.

Woods The skipper of the *New Hope*.

Kerdzic shrugs.

Don't bloody lie to me.

Kerdzic I'm not lying.

Beat.

Woods Let me see your pockets.

Kerdzic My pockets?

Woods Turn out your pockets.

Kerdzic I don't have to.

Woods Turn your pockets out, Kirk.

Kerdzic No.

Beat.

Woods You got something to hide?

Kerdzic No.

Woods You been taking things from this boat?

Kerdzic No.

Woods You been stealing?

Kerdzic I have not stolen anything.

Woods pulls the radio from his pocket.

Woods I found this on you.

Kerdzic No you didn't!

Woods In your pocket.

Kerdzic No. I'm standing here, you're standing over there and you took that from your pocket.

Woods You're a good bloke, Kirk, and I don't want you to spoil this trip for yourself. Tell me where they're headed.

Kerdzic I did not steal that.

Woods Where's the other boat?

Kerdzic I did not steal that. I did not take that.

Woods Answer the question, Kirk.

Kerdzic You're lying!

Woods Answer the question.

Kerdzic I am not a criminal!

Woods Just point on the map and we can forget all about this.

Kerdzic Help! Help me!

Woods Shut up, Kirk!

Kerdzic Help! Help!

Woods Kirk!

Kerdzic This is illegal, I am not a thief! Help!

Woods Kirk!

Kerdzic I have not stolen that!

Woods Alright, calm down . . .

Kerdzic Put it away! I'm not a criminal!

Woods Just calm down . . .

Kerdzic Help!

Woods Kirk!

Kerdzic Put it back!

Woods OK!

Kerdzic Put it back!

Woods I'm putting it back. I'm putting it back.

Kerdzic Away!

Woods (*pocketing the radio*) OK. It's gone. See, it's gone.

Kerdzic I am not a criminal. I don't know where the other boat is. The agency tells us nothing. We turn up on the dock with a paper in our hands.

  John enters.

John What's going on? Are you OK?

Pause.

Kerdzic I am not a criminal, John.

Kerdzic exits.

John What was that?

Woods Kirk's brother's a professional. He was meant to be with us. Matt paid more to get him. He knew we were coming out.

John He told you that? He looked upset.

Woods Leave the business side to me.

Pause.

John When was the last time you slept?

Woods I'm fine.

Exit.

> I dreamed a dream the other night,
> Lowlands, lowlands away my John,
> I dreamed a dream the other night,
> Lowlands, my lowlands away.

SCENE FIVE

The galley. Rhys and Graham in pinnies. Graham is busily preparing a meal over the kitchen surfaces. Rhys is stretching in preparation for his own contribution.

Rhys Eh, Graham, eh, big man, look at me go . . . like a bison . . . like a bison I am. Proper magic lunges going on over here, mate. You're missing out, son. You're missing out.

Graham I'm a little busy, Rhys.

Rhys Right you are. Big meal to prepare and that. I understand. Don't worry, Rhysie-boy's got your back, eh.

Graham Just do something useful! I'm under a lot of stress here.

Rhys Worry not, mate. I'm all over it. Like a rash I am, like a bloody great rash. I notice we've only got two spoons and three forks, what's going on there?

Graham WHAT!

Rhys Don't worry, mate, I'll find another spoon.

Graham It's knives we need!

Rhys Right you are. Knives it is. I'm on the hunt, Graham, don't you worry, I'm on the hunt. Rhys is on the hunt. Like a heat-seeking missile, I am. Knives, where are you, knives? I'm coming to find you! What's with these Christmas serviettes? We just changing things up a bit?

Graham It has to look proper, Rhys! Just find those bloody knives!

John enters unnoticed.

Rhys Knives it is, mate, don't panic, I'll take care of everything, taking care of business . . . Sod me, these are some good lunges going on. Eh, Graham, what do you think of these lunges I'm doing? Pretty grand, eh?

Graham RHYS!

John laughs. They notice him for the first time.

Rhys Alright, John!

John (*laughing*) What's this?

Rhys Big boys' meal, mate. Mackerel in a cheese sauce, with peas and diced carrots. And a can of Foster's.

43

John You cooked this?

Rhys He did.

John You?

Rhys Kitchen champion.

Graham You sound surprised?

John I didn't have you down as the culinary type. Anyway, I thought it was the Alan Special.

Graham Burger and chips is off the menu tonight.

John Marvellous.

John sits. Rhys takes on the mannerisms of a suave waiter.

Rhys Pepper, sir?

John Why, thank you.

Rhys (*bowing profusely*) My pleasure, sir, my pleasure. Would sir care for a glass and ice with his beverage?

John That would do nicely!

Alan enters. The charade drops abruptly.

Rhys (*subdued*) Get it yourself.

Alan moves towards the fridge. The others watch him. He takes a beer out and then moves towards the door.

Mackerel, Alan?

Alan ignores him and walks from the room.

Rhys We'll save you some then.

Kerdzic enters.

Graham Kirk!

Kerdzic Is Alan angry?

Rhys Just misunderstood.

John laughs.

Graham Look at that, my Polish friend. (*Presenting Kerdzic with a plate.*) Is that or is that not the best meal that you've seen in your sorry little life? Wouldn't be able to afford that back home, would you?

Rhys He's not poor, he's doing this to start a company.

John You're starting a company?

Kerdzic Cabs.

John Taxis.

Kerdzic Yes.

John Here or in Poland?

Kerdzic Warsaw.

Rhys That's in Poland, John.

John I know where Warsaw is.

Rhys Just checking.

Graham Stupid John.

Rhys Kirk, what do you make of the meal?

Kerdzic takes a bite out of the mackerel.

Kerdzic In Polish we would call this . . . food . . . that has already been eaten! But in English . . .

John and Rhys laugh. Kerdzic smiles.

Rhys Look how happy he is with himself!

John The word you're looking for is vomit!

Graham Shut up, John.

Kerdzic Thank you, Graham. It's the thought that counts.

Rhys Ouch.

Graham You're lucky I like you, Kirk!

Kerdzic The joke was funny.

John It was funny!

Graham If you don't like it you can leave it for Alan. I'm sure he'll gobble up those leftovers.

Rhys I think he jumped overboard.

Alan appears at the doorway, unobserved.

Kerdzic He is very angry. I saw him outside and he was crying. I asked if he was upset and if he wanted help and he told me to sod off back to Kazakhstan. This made me laugh because I am Polish and not Kazakhstanian, which is funny if you do not know the difference.

John I don't understand.

Graham Stupid John.

Kerdzic It's simple!

Graham It's simple, John!

Kerdzic They are different countries, John! Poland. Kazakhstan. Poland. Kazakhstan . . .

Laughter. They see Alan at the doorway. Laughter stops.

Rhys Hello, Alan. Nice of you to join us.

Alan sits.

Alan You have much experience on trawlers?

Kerdzic No.

Alan This is your first time out?

Kerdzic Yes. I am a virgin.

Brief laughter.

Alan You've been on boats before?

Kerdzic Yes. My brother was a fisherman in Poland.

Alan You went out with him?

Kerdzic Sometimes. His idea was come to England to do fishing.

Alan Were you ever out in a storm?

Kerdzic Yes.

Alan Tell me about it.

Rhys Alan.

Kerdzic I did not mean to offend you before.

Alan Tell me about the storm.

Kerdzic Well, it was windy and it was wet.

Rhys Never was a more accurate description given!

Alan How high were the waves?

Kerdzic They were high.

Alan In feet?

Kerdzic Feet?

Alan How high, in feet, were the waves?

Kerdzic I don't know.

Alan Did they break over the ship?

Kerdzic I don't . . .

Alan Simple question, did the waves fall on to the ship?

Kerdzic Yes.

Alan Did the ship capsize?

Kerdzic No.

Alan You ever been capsized?

Kerdzic No.

Alan John, you've been capsized, haven't you?

John Yes.

Alan You have, haven't you, Rhys?

Rhys You know me, can't stop myself.

Alan What force was this storm you were in?

Kerdzic I don't know.

Alan You ever been in a force ten?

Kerdzic I don't know.

Alan I doubt it. I have.

Graham Good for you.

Alan Do you mind? I was telling a story. Storm force ten, that's when you get forty-foot waves, big waves. And you're in this tiny can in the middle of it. The boat starts tumbling around, like this – (*He demonstrates with his hand.*) Like a tiny little thing. Metal and that, doesn't mean anything to the sea, if she want she'll just tear through it like ripping open an old scar. You can't stand up. Falling all over your mates, thrown across the room like you've been hit by car. Breaking bones on bulkheads. Crap falling out of them cupboards above you there. Even a frying pan can take your head off if it's got ten tonne of force behind it. Funny, isn't it? A frying pan. Some people get scared at this point, right? People sick themselves, some people . . . Then the windows shatter, you're looking at water, sheer water hitting glass head on, like a bus. That'll come straight out and if you're sat there when it happens then it'll shred you up. Skipper will be up there, fighting against the wheel. Both hands clinging to it, knuckles turning white. Fighting to turn into those waves, cutting through them with the bow. Because if one of those hills of water hits you side on then you're going under. That's when you get the darkness, just you and the depth.

They sit in silence.

(*Rising from his chair.*) I'll be upstairs.

Rhys Always glad of the update.

Alan exits.

John What was that about?

Beat.

Rhys His father, I think.

John Why?

Rhys (*gesturing at Graham*) This one.

John You're a bloody idiot sometimes, Graham.

Kerdzic What happened to his father?

Rhys Nothing of any importance. You handled yourself well there.

Exit.

> Sing away, we all drink whiskey and gin,
> Sing away, we're all dead drunk on the rum,
> Sing away, we all throw shit at the cook,
> Sing away, we'll pay Paddy Doyle for his boots.

SCENE SIX

*The galley. Night. Graham, John, Rhys, Alan and Kerdzic
enter from the deck. They are visibly tired as they remove
their wet-weather clothing, their movements heavy and
slow.*

Rhys It's getting choppy out there.

John It should pass soon, we're too far out for it to do us
any damage.

Graham Did you see the size of it? Looked like an
apocalypse.

Alan An apocalypse can only happen once, it would be
the apocalypse, not *an* apocalypse.

Graham The quality of conversation on this boat is
frightening.

John This isn't school, gentlemen, or the playground.

Graham Well, it'll be *the* apocalypse when we go inside.

John We're not going near any storms.

Graham Where do you think the fish are?

John They won't be in there.

Graham They're not in here.

John We'll catch something soon.

Graham (*noticing Kerdzic still in his wets*) Oi, Poseidon.
Get your gear off.

Kerdzic They are warm.

Rhys Didn't you bring more clothes?

Kerdzic No. My brother has them. He took them from
my bag. I'm very angry with him.

50

Rhys Mine's the same.

Kerdzic You have a brother?

Rhys Yes.

Kerdzic Does he steal from you?

Rhys And worse.

Kerdzic He beat you?

Graham Worse than that.

Kerdzic He tried to kill you?

Graham Almost.

Rhys He introduced me to my wife.

Kerdzic You don't love her?

Rhys I married her.

Kerdzic I don't understand.

John Neither does he.

Rhys You're one to talk.

Kerdzic You are married also?

John I was married.

Beat.

Kerdzic She is dead?

Graham He wishes.

John No, she's not dead. She lives in Brixham. She got remarried.

Kerdzic Do you see her around?

John Most days.

Kerdzic With her husband?

John Sometimes.

Kerdzic No, no . . . She is a female dog! Have you ever fought him?

John A couple of times.

Graham No, you haven't.

Kerdzic I would fight him. Why do you not find a new woman? That would make her angry. You should do that.

John I'm not interested any more. I spend too much time out here. I don't want to make her angry.

Kerdzic You still upset by her?

John Not out here.

Graham John thinks the whole town is laughing at him.

John No I don't!

Rhys Ignore him.

Graham It's true, he said it!

John I never!

Rhys Jesus, some sensitivity from you wouldn't go amiss!

John I never said that! I only said that I overheard people talking, that was it!

Rhys It's alright, John.

John I never said that!

Rhys I know.

Kerdzic You should find a new woman.

John I don't know, I think I'm past it now.

Rhys Nonsense! You're not even forty!

John I don't think I'm what your average woman is looking for.

Rhys That's outrageous.

Graham Outrageous.

Rhys That's outrageous.

Graham Outrageous.

Rhys You live in a semi-detached house. You're divorced. You make a modest income. You drive a Citroën.

Graham Your name's John.

Rhys You're the definition of average man! You're exactly what an average woman is looking for!

John Well, maybe when I get back I'll put out the feelers.

Graham explodes with laughter.

Graham You'll what?

Rhys Look at Casanova! Spreading his feelers around the bosoms of Brixham!

John Alright, alright.

John tries to calm Graham, who is now in hysterics.

Kerdzic Alan, do you have a wife?

Graham, Rhys and John look at Alan.

Alan You're awfully chatty, aren't you?

Kerdzic I am sorry.

Pause.

Alan Her name is Susan. We got married at eighteen. I've never been with another woman.

Beat.

Kerdzic Is she pretty?

Alan Yes.

Beat.

Kerdzic What does she look like?

Alan She has black hair down to about here – (*Indicates below the ear.*) Grey lines struck through it like someone's drawn it with a pencil. She wears it up most of the time, in a knot back here – (*Indicates the back of the head.*) She likes those Japanese sticks, they're short about yay and she puts it in and twists it round or something like that. I don't know how it works.

Kerdzic Do you miss her when you are out here?

Alan Yes. Very much. I bloody hate her sometimes.

Laughter.

Rhys Amen. I knew that was coming.

Woods' voice barks from the intercom.

Woods They're pinging everywhere, we've got pings.

Rhys Here we go!

John On deck.

Kerdzic What are pings?

Alan Sonar bouncing off fish, lots of fish.

They all struggle to get their wet-weather clothes on. Kerdzic already has his on, and is standing quite calmly, waiting for the others.

Graham Let's go!

Kerdzic Does Woods have a wife?

Alan What?

John Graham, get him outside!

Graham I'm putting my jacket on.

In his urgency Rhys trips and falls. Grabbing at everything on his way down, he pulls Alan to the floor. They land in a compromising heap.

Rhys Alan, what have I told you about grabbing me in front of the other boys? It's just not cricket.

Laughter from Graham as he struggles with his own wets. Rhys and Alan are finding it difficult to get to their feet.

Are you like this with Susan?

Alan Someone help me!

Rhys I'm not wearing protection, Alan . . .

Graham We've got a man overboard, get in there, Kirk!

Woods' voice comes over the intercom.

Woods Where is everyone?

John manages to lift Alan and then Rhys. They bundle towards the door, still half dressed. Woods' voice erupts again.

Wait! Wait. Stay where you are. It's gone. I'm not getting anything. It's all empty. This equipment is useless! John, get up here.

Exit.

Leave her Johnny, leave her.
Leave her Johnny, leave her.
For the voyage is done,
And the winds don't blow
And it's time for us to leave her.

The wheelhouse. Woods is bent over a mass of charts, studying them in detail. John enters.

John Did you see?

Woods Yes.

John The other net nearly went. Half of it's all frayed up. I doubt we've got another go with her.

   Beat.

(*Gesturing at the map.*) You taking us home?

   Beat.

Woods Come here.

   John joins him at the table.

Look at this. We're down here, just south of that. Now, if we go north-west there's all these trenches here. Matt won't touch that and it's prime ground.

John Wind speed?

   Beat.

Woods Fifty knots.

   Beat.

John Mean or gust?

Woods Mean.

John Close on eleven.

Woods The *Hope* won't go there. Matt's too afraid. With luck he's struggling same as we are. Anywhere else is fair game for him. We can't compete. But if we get in along there, get a good catch quick and hoof it back . . .

John Or turn back.

Pause.

Woods I'm not losing another boat, John. I won't crawl back and have them laugh at me. I'm not doing it. We're going further out.

John They won't like it.

Beat.

Woods Can you tell them?

John It should be you.

Woods I thought this was an equal partnership?

John is silent.

Bring them up.

John exits. Woods stands by himself. The whole crew enter, except Alan.

OK, right . . . where's Alan?

Alan appears at the doorr, hesitant to enter.

Alan I think I'll stay below.

Woods No, you all need to hear this.

John It'll only be a couple of minutes.

Beat.

Alan Two minutes. And then I'm going back down.

Alan slowly enters the room.

Graham Do you want someone to hold your hand?

Alan Stop staring at me.

Woods waits till he arrives.

Woods You've all done strong work so far and I'm sorry it's not come through for us. But we've still got some options. I've just been over the charts with John, and he's agreed that if we go a bit further out . . .

Graham How far?

John Let him finish.

Graham Which direction?

Rhys Ease off, Graham.

Graham Which bloody way?

Kerdzic North-west.

Beat.

Graham He knows. North-west. Right into that storm. I told you, Rhys, didn't I bloody tell you?

Woods We don't have a choice.

Graham No. All I hear from you is that I don't have a choice. You've said that about everything. You said that about coming out and I had a choice then. Sod it, I don't even know if you're going to pay me. We go back.

Graham walks towards the door.

Alan Coward.

Beat.

Graham Come on then, old man.

Graham runs at Alan. Before he can get there John and Rhys have stepped between. Woods pulls him away.

Woods Graham!

Graham I'll kick your head in, mate!

Woods Let it go.

Graham Dick!

Woods Let it go. If you want to go for someone, go for me. It's my fault we're here.

Graham Get off me!

Woods You can sound off about your feelings, Graham, and all those grand things you could be doing, but you're still here and there are lads here that don't have what you have. They don't have a choice. Sod the rest of it, but you respect that.

   Pause.

I've asked a lot of you all over the years, and I know I'm asking for more now. We started this company with one boat. At its height we had fifteen vessels fully manned. Fifteen boats. A fleet. We had more money than we knew what to do with. Remember that? The only risk we had was what might happen to us out here. Now I don't know if it was the naivety of youth. Recklessness, indifference perhaps. It's different now. We're further down the line and maybe I'm looking back through tinted glasses, but there's something that's been lost. Something that slipped between our fingers. It can be salvaged here. We're back at the start. One bloody boat and three stinking nets. And I'm not prepared to leave this one empty-handed. We've come too far now to finish on empty. If we get out ahead of the *Hope*, there's trenches that Matt won't shoot line into. I know him. He's too afraid. He's got a big ship, yes. He's faster, yes. But he doesn't have the balls to go headlong into that. If we can get out there, get one good run and back. It's ours.

   Pause.

Rhys It's hasty.

Woods It's prime ground.

Rhys There's no guarantee of a catch.

John There's never guarantees.

Rhys We're not in great shape. We're short on nets.

John Structurally she will hold. I've been over the engines today and she can handle it. Three nets is enough.

Rhys Has she ever been out in anything like this before? For that matter how many of us have?

John The boat will hold, Rhys.

Alan What would happen if we turned . . . ?

Woods No pay. No back pay. Boat will be sold, although that will probably happen anyway. The girls will go without pay.

    Beat.

Rhys What strength is it?

Woods About a nine.

    Beat.

Rhys Eighty-kilometre winds? Seven-metre waves?

Woods Predicted.

Rhys So it could go higher.

Woods It could go lower, that's what's predicted. I promise you we can get fish. We can all go our separate ways after this.

    Pause.

Graham Double pay?

    A spattering of laughter.

Well, you didn't bloody pay us for the last one.

Woods You'll have everything we make off this, there's no other money.

Graham What about Kirk?

Woods He's on agency pay.

Graham If he's coming with us, he deserves equal.

Beat.

Woods OK.

Graham You want a bung, Kirk?

Kerdzic I don't take bribes.

Graham It's not a bribe, Kirk. Take the money.

Kerdzic I will take the money.

Pause.

Woods I think we're done here?

Pause.

This is good news, lads. The nets need to be cleared and after that I suggest you get your heads down.

The crew exit. Rhys lingers for a moment and then leaves. John and Woods are left standing by themselves.

Say it.

John is silent.

Go on, say it, we're old friends.

John I'm done.

Woods Don't get heavy with me, John. You can't carry it off.

John You said it was a nine, when you know it's eleven.

Woods Predicted eleven.

John They have a right to know.

Woods They wouldn't understand.

John Alan's seen more storms than either of us and Rhys has been around.

Woods There's more at stake at here.

John Sixty-foot waves.

Woods They'll get frightened.

John They should be.

Woods If they get frightened they won't think about it clearly, it's better for them this way.

John Don't say you're doing it for them.

Woods I'm doing this for myself, am I?

John If this had anything to do with them, you wouldn't have lied.

Beat.

Woods I remember, John . . . I remember this man. This man, coming to my door in the middle of the night. Coming to my house, my home, crying. Crying, saying he had nothing and asking for my help. She'd done one and taken everything. You must remember that, John? Surely you must remember that? And do you remember what I did then?

Beat.

What did I do then, John?

John Woods . . .

Woods I put you up, didn't I. Took you in and got you back on your feet. When you had nothing left you came to me and I put you up. And that ain't the first time I've pulled you up, is it, John? Ain't the first bloody time I can remember, and it probably won't be the last, will it? You want me to go back through the other ones?

John Is the company worth this much to you?

Woods Shut your bloody mouth, John! You're a bloody coward! This company has provided for us all. This company's given you everything you've got! I didn't hear any complaints when the money was flooding into your pockets.

John All profit, is it?

Woods The company is dead, John!

John Pride, then? You'll sink us for your own pride? Here's the man that can't be proved wrong.

Woods This is why she left you, John. Because you could never risk – you could have had your own boat by now, and you know it, but you were too afraid of achieving. You don't have the balls to do this job and I won't carry you any longer.

John Fine.

Woods Good.

John You know your wife left you too. And she left you because you were an arrogant, manipulative . . .

Woods Yes?

John Bully.

Pause. Woods laughs.

Woods That the best you can do, John? Christ, it's worse than I thought.

John When we get back I'm done, this is just business from now on.

Woods Still wanting to make a penny out of it then?

John I mean it, I'm gone.

Silence. They've run out of words.

Woods Get on deck.

The two school friends watch as what is left of their friendship passes away. John exits, Woods is left alone.

> Hand, hand, hand over hand.
> Never run away with a Liverpool man.
> Hand, hand, hand over hand.
> Never run away with a Liverpool man.

SCENE EIGHT

The deck. John and Graham. Large floodlights break the darkness and illuminate the boat as it rocks heavily. Waves are breaking on to the deck.

John Graham! Pull those nets in!

No response.

Graham! Pull the bloody nets in!

Again no response.

Graham! Graham! Graham!

Graham What!

John Why didn't you answer?

Graham I was ignoring you!

Pause.

John Graham!

Graham What! Bloody hell! What!

64

John Pull those nets in!

Graham Do it yourself!

John Pull those nets in!

Graham Pull those nets in, pull those nets, bloody whiney . . .

John Alan's right about you! I've tried to defend you to him, but he's right!

Graham Alan's an old lanky . . .

The net is hauled in and hangs above them. It is clearly bursting with fish. John is speechless. Graham is still operating the machinery and hasn't noticed, he continues to berate John.

John Graham!

Graham I've pulled them in, John!

John We've bloody got them!

John staggers to Graham and embraces him.

We've bloody well got them!

John turns Graham and points to the net.

Graham Fish . . .

Beat.

John / Graham Fish!

Graham (*to wheelhouse*) Woods! We've done it!

John and Graham laugh and embrace again as Rhys, Alan and Kerdzic enter. They stare at the catch.

John / Graham Fish!

Beat.

John / Graham / Rhys / Alan / Kerdzic Fish!

They turn to the wheelhouse.

John / Graham / Rhys / Alan / Kerdzic Fish!

They laugh and embrace again.

John Pull the other net in!

Graham kicks the machine into action.

Graham Second one coming in.

A second net is pulled over the side. It has an even larger haul than the first. They cheer, laugh and embrace.

Rhys Is the other one out?

Graham Bringing her in now!

Graham cheers again, he slaps Kerdzic on the back. The third net falls heavily on to the deck, brimming with fish. They share their congratulations with the wheelhouse.

Rhys You beautiful . . .

John Let's go home!

Exit.

SCENE NINE

The galley. Rhys, Graham, Woods, Alan and Kerdzic.

Alan (*sings*)
>   Says she who like a sailor, now see me more
>   you may,
>   But when we reached her padded shore she
>   this to me did say . . .

All (*sing*)

>Well then away you santy, my dear Annie.
>Oh you New York girls can't you dance the
>>polka.

Rhys / Graham (*falsetto*)

>My flashman he's a Yankee, with his hair cut
>>short behind.
>He wears a pair of long sea boots and he sails
>>in the butterball line.
>He's homeward bound to see me, and when
>>we meet he'll say,
>So get a move, young sailor boy, get cracking
>>on your way.

All

>Then away you santy, my dear Annie.
>Oh you New York girls can't you dance the
>>polka.

Alan

>So I kissed her hard and proper, afore her
>>flashman came.
>And fairly well me married girl I know your
>>little game!

All

>Well then away you santy, my dear Annie.
>Oh you New York girls can't you dance the
>>polka.

*The number reaches its finale. They cheer and drink.
John's voice crackles over the intercom.*

John Woods?

Rhys He's down here!

John Woods!

Woods What?

John Get up here.

Woods What's on?

Woods exits.

Alan Silly buggers.

Kerdzic That is a great song.

Pause.

Graham Oi, John!

No response.

What's going on?

The intercom crackles into life, it struggles for a second and then appears to die, silence. Faintly Woods' voice can be heard.

Woods *New Hope?*

Pause.

New Hope, this is the *Violet*. Give your last again . . .

Pause.

New Hope, this is the *Violet*. Say your last again . . . Matt?

Pause.

Matt, it's Woods, give us your last again, we need your position. Over.

Matt (*broken staccato transmission*) This is the *New Hope* . . . All vessels in area . . . we . . . in urgent . . .

The signal fades.

Woods Matt, say again.

Signal slowly returns.

Matt . . . Overboard . . . assistance . . . ten . . . passing . . . 5 . . . 9 . . . 5.

The intercom dies.

Rhys Bloody thing!

Graham John, we've lost it down here!

The intercom crackles into life one final time.

Matt . . . Force eleven . . . all vessels urgent assistance . . .

The signal dies.

Woods Matt?

Beat.

Matt. If you can hear me, hold tight. We're informing coastguard. *Violet* out.

The intercom dies. The crew stand in silence. Graham becomes aware of Kerdzic.

Graham Kirk?

The others look towards him. He is frozen.

Are you alright, mate?

Kerdzic is whispering in Polish.

Kirk . . .

Kerdzic's mumbling becomes louder and more confused. He finds clarity and his eyes dart up, catching Graham's.

Kerdzic Jozef.

Kerdzic runs towards the wheelhouse. The others move to stop him.

Jozef is on that boat . . .

Graham I know . . .

Kerdzic We have to get Jozef now!

Woods enters.

Jozef!

Woods It's alright, Kirk. It's alright. The coastguard are on their way.

Rhys Easy, mate.

Graham Don't worry, we're going to get him.

Woods No we are not.

Beat.

Graham You're going to leave them out there?

Woods My first priority is this ship and this crew.

Alan How are we meant to help them? We're going to pull up alongside and they're going to jump across?

Woods There's seventy-mile an hour winds, we'd be no use.

Beat.

Graham Vote.

Woods This isn't a democracy.

Graham Now it is.

Woods It's a company and I'm your boss!

Graham Sod the company.

Woods We're going home.

Graham Those who want to go, raise hands.

Kerdzic and Graham raise their hands.

Alan Put your hands down.

Graham Rhys?

Rhys You want to go?

Graham We have to.

Alan This isn't right!

Rhys You understand how dangerous this is?

Woods Rhys!

Rhys You said it was a nine.

Pause.

Graham What?

Woods That's what was predicted.

Rhys You never were a good liar, Woods.

Beat.

You did it, mate. I didn't. You did. We may have pulled that net in, but you took us there. You were right.

Beat.

We can't leave them. You know that.

Rhys raises his hand.

Graham Three against two.

Rhys John hasn't voted.

Graham John!

John's voice echoes down.

John Busy.

Graham We need your vote – do we go to the *Hope* or do we leave?

John We're voting?

Graham New development.

John What's the vote so far?

Graham It doesn't matter, John.

John Yes it does, I want to know.

Graham Three–two.

John Which way?

Graham Going.

   Beat.

John You should know it's force eleven.

Graham We know.

John I wanted to say . . .

Rhys Vote, John.

   Beat.

John Go.

Rhys Four–two.

   Beat.

Alan So it's done? You've all had your voting and now I have to go?

Woods You know what will happen?

Rhys Moral obligation and that.

Woods I hope you've got strong shoulders.

Alan You're taking this decision for me?

Graham We've voted.

Alan I haven't. I've no death wish. You don't even know what you're going to do when we get there. I'm not going to be told by an emotional teenager and some fair-weather Polish monkey that my life is forfeit because they suddenly grew a pair!

Rhys If the history of this job is built on anything, then it's the hundreds of men, sons, fathers and brothers that have risked for each other out there. We take that risk every time we come out. That's the difference. Some of us had a choice to be here, others didn't. Life's shit like that. But I'll tell you something else, life's a lot shitter for a group of men no different from ourselves, no different from you, that are out there, alone, in the swell. These men will cry and scream for help. No different from you. And when none comes the water will fill their lungs. No different than yours. And when they scream, they're screaming at you. Now, if you want to turn, you turn your back on everything that you've been holding on to out here in this job, because all it is, is them.

Pause.

Alan No . . .

Beat.

We won't come back.

Graham We're wasting time.

Graham turns to exit.

Alan Not like this.

Graham Save it.

Woods Graham.

Beat. Graham stops.

I'll take it.

Woods moves past Graham to exit.

Alan We don't have to do it. We can still turn back. No one will know.

Rhys We will.

Graham, Rhys and Kerdzic move quickly to strike the chairs.

Alan I can't . . . no. You foolish . . .

John enters.

John Come away from the windows.

John pulls Alan towards the centre. They all reach out to steady the table as the boat rocks.

Graham My mother would kill me.

A splattering of laughter. The light above them swings from side to side. They stare at it. The intercom crackles into life.

Woods Turning due west.

Pause.

Brace.

A small shudder passes through the ship as a wave breaks along the side. Silence again.

John Everyone good?

Mumbled responses.

We'll need to throw line when we get close. Tie rings to the end and get them into the water. Two to a line. Graham and Rhys together. (*To Kerdzic.*) I'm with you. We go in shifts. They're going to get worse, so . . .

Woods Brace.

Wave strikes.

Graham Christ.

Alan This is all wrong.

Beat.

Graham You alright there, Kirk?

Kerdzic nods. Silence.

Rhys There are two waves out in the ocean.

They all look at Rhys.

Two waves. Big wave, and a little wave. Now the little wave, he's having a ball of a time, throwing himself about. When he looks out ahead of him and sees all these other waves breaking across the shore . . .

Woods Brace.

A more violent wave breaks on the ship.

Rhys The little wave . . . the little wave, he turns to the bigger with eyes wide and heart heavy. And the bigger wave looks right back at him and says, 'I know what your problem is. You were having so much fun being a wave, you forgot you were just part of the ocean.'

Beat. Some laughter.

Woods They're in the water.

Beat.

Alan We shouldn't be here.

Beat.

Rhys Let's go, boyo.

Rhys and Graham prepare to leave.

John No, we'll go first. You ready?

Kerdzic Ready.

John As soon as we come in, you go out. No matter what happens, no one goes in. Gentlemen.

Rhys We'll see you out there.

John and Kerdzic exit.

This is it.

Silence.

Woods I can see them.

Alan God help us . . .

Rhys Steady now, boys.

Woods I'll come down to one-quarter speed, but you'll have to move fast, we can't stay dead in the water.

Beat.

Alan No, that's too slow.

Rhys Alan, it's OK . . .

Woods Slowing.

Alan No. Don't go below half, we can't stay steady.

Beat.

Woods Half-speed . . .

Alan No!

Beat.

Rhys Woods!

Beat.

Woods!

Woods I'm turning in now . . .

Alan That's too slow! We can't turn at that speed!

Woods Turning.

Rhys Woods!

Beat.

Woods Stand by.

Alan Woods!

Rhys Brace!

A thunderous wave breaks across the ship, throwing everyone apart. A cry from Woods signals a sudden roar from the engines and the ship breaks free. Alan runs to the doorway, calling up to Woods.

Woods Christ, that was big.

Alan Give her power!

Woods We've come in too slow.

Rhys Woods!

Alan Give her everything now! Pull us out.

Woods I can't. There's no power.

Alan (*to Rhys*) Engines are flooded . . .

Woods We're going to collide!

Rhys (*calling him to the table*) Alan!

Alan moves back to the table. Kerdzic appears.

Woods Away from the windows!

Graham Kirk!

Woods Brace!

The two ships collide. Kerdzic is knocked off his feet. Rhys and Graham rush towards him. Darkness. We hear Rhys and Graham struggling.

Graham Bloody hell, Kirk.

Rhys Put pressure on it.

Graham Kirk, you alright?

Rhys Where's John?

Kerdzic The bodies . . .

Rhys Get us light.

Alan finds a torch, illuminating the scene. Kerdzic unconscious on the table, Graham and Rhys attending to him.

Is John still outside?

Graham He's pissing blood, mate.

Kerdzic John went in . . .

Graham John's in the water?

Woods Turning!

Kerdzic I couldn't do anything, he fell in. John . . .

Rhys It's alright, mate.

Alan We need to turn back.

Woods Stand by!

Rhys Hold him.

They gather over him.

Woods Brace.

A wave breaks. They are forced to the floor. The torch goes out. Darkness. Muffled sounds of a struggle.

Graham Come on.

Rhys Get him back on the table.

Woods I've got no steering up here, John.

Rhys Hold him.

Woods John! I'm not getting any power.

Alan He's bleeding everywhere . . .

Woods Where's John?

Rhys Alan. Tell him.

Alan I'm not going up there.

Woods John!

Rhys Go!

Alan Get off me!

The sound of a struggle. Flesh colliding with flesh.
Silence. A red flare is lit illuminating the scene,
Graham and Rhys are attending to Kirk.

Graham Alan?

Rhys He's topside.

Graham Kirk's not doing well, mate.

Woods enters.

Woods Where is he?

Rhys Overboard.

Woods You let him go . . .

Rhys I wasn't there.

Woods He went alone?

Rhys He was with Kirk.

Woods begins to remove his wets.

What are you doing?

Woods I'm going for John.

Woods removes his jacket and boots.

Rhys We can't get you back.

Woods I know.

Rhys Woods . . .

Woods I can't leave him, Rhys.

Beat.

Bring us home.

Woods exits. Alan's voice crackles over the speaker.

Alan I can't do this.

Graham He's not looking good.

Alan There's no power. I can't do this.

Rhys Stay with it, Alan!

Alan I can't . . . I'm sorry . . .

Rhys Alan!

Alan I'm sorry.

Rhys Brace.

The boat turns sharply and they are rocked by another massive wave accompanied by a deafening smashing sound.

The water's coming in.

Graham Alan?

Rhys See if he's alright.

Graham exits.

Don't worry Kirk, we'll be out of here in no time.

Beat.

God, if you let me get home I promise I will speak to my wife again.

Graham re-enters.

Alan?

Graham The glass smashed . . .

Rhys Alan?

Graham . . .

Rhys Come here.

Graham He needs a hospital.

Rhys There's not any near.

> *Beat.*

Graham Are we going to die?

> *Pause.*

Say we're not going to die.

> *Beat.*

I'm scared. Are you scared?

Rhys Yes.

Graham What do we do?

> *Beat.*

I don't want to do this any more.

> *Beat.*

I don't want to die like my dad. I'm scared.

> *Beat.*

It's OK to die. It's OK to die. It's OK to die. I don't want to die.

Rhys It will be OK.

Graham I want to live. I really want to live, please don't let me die. I'm scared, Rhys, I'm really scared.

Rhys It's OK.

Graham Oh God. God help me. Please God, please. I'm scared.

Rhys We're not going anywhere. We're not going anywhere.

Graham I can't breathe.

Rhys It's just us, mate.

Graham Oh my God. Save me.

Rhys It's just me and you.

Graham Save me.

Rhys I can't. I can't.

Beat.

Graham Is this it?

Rhys . . .

Graham Is this it?

Pause.

Rhys Graham, I can't swim. Don't tell anyone.

Graham Neither can I.

They laugh. Look up. Listen. Rhys pulls Graham towards him

Rhys Good luck.

A wave crashes against the ship, forcing it to roll over. They are capsized. Darkness.

The cast sing from 'The Last Leviathan' by Andy Barnes.

End.